GO FO

The S

The Story Continues...

RICHARD FENTON &
ANDREA WALTZ

Published by
SUCCESS IN 10 PAGES
SHORT BOOKS. BIG IDEAS.

ISBN 978-1-947814-33-2

NOTE FROM THE AUTHORS

It's hard to believe that 25 years have passed since the release of our original book, "Go for No!" What started as a simple idea—encouraging people to embrace rejection as a steppingstone to success—has grown into a movement that has impacted millions around the world.

When we first wrote "Go for No!" we had no idea how far it would go or how deeply it would resonate. But after 25 years and over 1 million copies sold, plus translations in a dozen languages, we knew there was more to be said, more to be shared, and new lessons to explore.

This book is a deeper dive into the mindset of success, packed with insights gathered from a lifetime of speaking, training and practicing the principles that have guided us for the past quarter-century.

Over the years, we've seen the world change. The landscape of business has shifted with technology, and with the rise of AI, things are about to shift even more. However, one thing that we believe will continue as a grounding principle of success is a willingness to fail.

If anything, the last 25 years have reinforced our belief that the most successful people, whether in sales, business, or life, are the ones who understand that:

1. Failure is not the enemy of success, it's the foundation, and...
2. Rejection is not a sign to turn back—it's a signal to dig deeper, grow stronger, and move forward with even more determination.

In this sequel, we're excited to share what has been

happening to Eric Bratton since he had the supernatural opportunity to meet his future self and learn that the secret to his success had been the willingness to hear 'no' more often. Now, the Bratton Family has a big dream, one that will challenge them to become their most courageous selves.

To everyone who has been with us on this journey, thank you. Your stories, your courage, and your willingness to share your experiences have been the inspiration behind this book. Whether you read the original book many years ago or are just discovering the philosophy for the first time, we hope this sequel brings you new insights, new motivation and a renewed commitment to chasing your goals despite fear.

With Gratitude,

Richard Fenton & Andrea Waltz
Orlando, Florida · March 2025

FOREWORD BY DR. BENJAMIN HARDY

When I first listened to the Go for No! audiobook, it was one of those rare books that literally compelled me to action.

I was in a tricky spot in my business. I was in a partnership that absolutely had run its course, but I was not yet courageous enough to either: 1) reset the deal so it was more aligned, or 2) walk away.

Well, Go for No! hit me so hard that I couldn't even finish it before taking one of the boldest actions of my life. At that time, my neighborhood was a one-mile loop. I was about a third of a mile away from my house, walking in the opposite direction, when I had to turn around and sprint home!

I sprinted home and sent the most direct and honest email of my life. I "went for no," knowing a "no" wouldn't be the worst potential outcome. No, the worst potential outcome would be continuing to be where I then was.

At least with "no," I could move on to the next. At least with "no," I'd no longer be running circles in my head wondering *"what if?"*

Go for No! liberated me from "no." It stopped being an obstacle to avoid and instead, a rite of passage each time I wanted to grow.

Going for no is a way of life. If you're willing to embrace it, you can swing for the fences. What's the worst that can happen? Oh, you get a "no?"

I'm applying Go for No! at my company, SCALING.COM, to get the world's biggest leaders and entrepreneurs to work with us—

to partner with us, helping us scale the world.

Go for No! is one of those rare books that can actually change your life, if you just apply it. And apply it A LOT!!!!

I'm so glad we are now getting a follow-up to this classic book. And in this new follow-up, you will find how to apply "no" at the absolute highest level. Mark my words, you're about to get a masterclass in performance psychology and scaling.

Do you want to achieve the seemingly impossible? Then read this book as fast as you possibly can! Maybe, like me, you won't even be able to finish what you're doing before you make the boldest move of your life!

Dr. Benjamin Hardy, co-founder of SCALING.COM
and author of *THE SCIENCE OF SCALING*

Orlando, Florida · March 2025

"Choose your future, or it will choose you."

-Richard Fenton & Andrea Waltz

CARLSBAD, CALIFORNIA
TWENTY-FIVE YEARS LATER

Eric James Bratton sat at a small table on the balcony overlooking the seventh green at the La Costa Resort Golf Course and sipped his coffee. It was a beautiful, crystal clear morning, with the kind of sky so blue it almost hurt your eyes.

A lot had happened since he fell through the wormhole 25 years earlier and met his future self. His once mediocre sales career flourished. He became Vice President of Sales at CopyQuest. He wrote a best-selling book and became an in-demand professional speaker.

Which presented a problem.

"You've got to make a decision, Eric," the CEO said. *"Do you want to be a professional speaker, or do you want to help run this company? You can't do both."*

He was right, of course.

A choice had to be made.

As much as Eric loved his career, delivering the "Go for No!" message to a wider audience was more important. So, he left and launched a company dedicated to spreading his sales and management philosophies to the world. Not only had he made more money than he ever imagined, but the mission of helping others fulfilled him in a way he could never have predicted.

Plus, he'd been married to his wonderful wife, Elaine, for 28 years. And he owned the spectacular house from his mystical four-day trip to a parallel universe. He had lived into the vision of his future self.

Everyone thought Eric had simply dreamed up the *other him* after hitting his head on the nightstand and slipping into a coma. He wasn't so sure. It felt too real.

Some things turned out differently, though. Sadly, his brother, Carl, died of a heart attack at the age of 47, and unlike the other him, he and Elaine had been blessed with a fantastic daughter named Cassidy, who was about to graduate from college.

* * *

Eric padded quietly down the hallway toward his office, careful not to wake Elaine, who was a notoriously light sleeper. He marveled at the woman she had become, a transformation that was every bit as radical as his own.

The year Eric met his future self, Elaine owned a successful art gallery in San Diego's historic Gaslamp Quarter. A decade later, Elaine launched her own company, the Elaine Bratton Galleries, establishing itself as a major player in the contemporary art market.

The engine that made the galleries thrive was the carefully trained sales team at each location. No one walked out of one of Elaine's galleries without saying "no" at least once.

And then there was Cassidy.

Like her parents, she was scrappy. Unfortunately, Cassidy had trouble deciding what to do with her gifts.

Eric knew that beneath her confident exterior, Cassidy was often caught between wanting to make them proud and forging her own path, often leading to self-doubt and hesitation. Her perfectionist tendencies sometimes left her paralyzed, afraid to make mistakes or take risks that might lead to failure.

Eric had preached the benefits of increasing her failure rate, but she hadn't taken to the idea.

A standout golfer in high school, Cassidy played competitively for two years at the University of Southern California before stepping away from the sport. Even though she had left the team, her skill and love for the game remained a big part of who she was.

Now, Cassidy was graduating from USC.

Eric entered his office and made his way to his desk, not bothering to turn on the lights, and plugged his portable projector into his laptop. A second later, the wall was filled with images: a lush green golf course, clubhouse, cocktail lounge, stocked pro shop, upscale locker room, boutique hotel with private terraces, spa services, and an intimate resort-style pool. There were also photos of Eric playing golf with some of the world's biggest celebrities and professional golfers.

Eric leaned back and gazed at the images, letting the visions seep into his mind. He was determined to buy the Strawberry Creek Golf Course, where his time travel experience had happened, and restore it to the excellence it had been once upon a time.

It was a dream he could not let go of. Then again, maybe the dream wouldn't let go of him.

Chapter One
GRADUATION

Cassidy Bratton fidgeted nervously in a line of graduates donned in black caps and gowns at the edge of the stage in the sprawling University of Southern California courtyard.

The weight of four years spent working through late-night study sessions, challenging projects and self-doubt flooded her mind. Her future was a blank slate, full of opportunities, yet shrouded in uncertainty. When this day came, she thought she'd know what she would do with her life. Instead, she didn't have a clue.

Cassidy's trance was broken when her name echoed through the loudspeaker. She started across the stage, her black gown swirling around her legs and the little bundle threads from her tassel lightly brushing her cheek.

The University of Southern California was a private school in Los Angeles, known for business, engineering, and communications, and widely recognized for its excellent film school.

It wasn't cheap.

Not that her parents couldn't afford it. They could. Cassidy had never questioned whether they would pay her way or even asked about the cost; they were simply thrilled that she had been accepted. But when one of her friends told her that tuition, housing, meals, and books came to $85,000 per year, Cassidy almost passed out.

Now that she was graduating, the pressure to make their investment in her pay off grew daily.

Cassidy glanced toward the crowd and spotted her father and mother's proud faces. Cassidy smiled, her anxiety melting away as she shook the dean's hand and accepted the diploma. This was supposed to be the crowning moment of her life, yet she felt lost. She could almost hear her father's voice in her head: *"So, what are your plans now, Cass?"*

It was a good question for which she had no answer. She knew she needed to come up with one soon. It was almost certain to be the focus of conversation at dinner that night.

Chapter Two

MAYBE I COULD WORK FOR YOU?

Eric, Elaine, and Cassidy rode the elevator up to Bertrand at Mister A's on their way to celebrate Cassidy's graduation.

One of San Diego's most iconic fine-dining establishments, Mister A's was perched on a building rooftop in the Bankers Hill neighborhood and featured a stunning panoramic view of downtown San Diego, Balboa Park, and the San Diego Bay.

The maître d' escorted them to their regular table along the window where they could watch the airplanes land at San Diego International Airport. "This is nice, Dad. Thank you. You, too, Mom," Cassidy said. "I don't suppose we can get a bottle of champagne?"

"This is your night, sweetie," Elaine said. "Whatever you want."

"Absolutely!" Eric said. "It's not every day your daughter graduates from college magna cum laude. We couldn't be prouder of you, kiddo."

Everyone took a moment to scan the menu, which was completely unnecessary since they all knew they were having the same dishes they always ordered.

After the entrees had been consumed, Cassidy grew increasingly nervous. The question was coming, and she dreaded having to answer it. As if on cue, her father turned to her and said, "So, what have you decided?"

"I'm thinking cheesecake," Cassidy quipped, knowing full well the question had nothing to do with dessert.

"Seriously, Cass," Elaine said. "You've got to choose a direction for your life. You can move back home while you figure things out, of course."

"Well, I do have one idea," Cassidy said.

"Really? That's great," Eric said. "What are you thinking?"

"I was thinking maybe I could come work for you," Cassidy said cautiously.

"Work for *me*?" Eric asked.

"Yes, in the family business," Cassidy said.

"There is no family business anymore," Elaine said. "Your father decided to stop speaking and get off the road this year."

"Your mom wants me home," Eric said, "And I agree. It's time. I'm practically retired, anyway. There really isn't any way to put you to work."

Cassidy fell silent. There was nothing she could think of saying. There was only one thing to do now. Have another glass of champagne.

Chapter Three

A PLAN FOR CASSIDY

Eric sat behind his desk and gazed at the images of his golf course dream. Admittedly, no vision board could come close to the experience of falling into a parallel universe and seeing himself as successful. Vision boards were the next best method he'd come across.

A few seconds later, he heard Elaine's footsteps coming down the hallway. Eric leaned forward and hit the projector's off-button.

"Hey, what's up?" Eric asked when she appeared in the doorway.

"I was wondering what you were thinking about Cassidy."

"I don't know. I wish she had something she wanted to work toward, but..."

"Her friends Chloe and Ruwan want her to backpack across Europe with them," Elaine said.

"What? Like for the summer?"

"No, for a year," Elaine said.

"Not a chance," Eric said, shaking his head.

"You don't trust her?"

"Oh, I trust Cassidy plenty," Eric said. "It's the rest of the world I don't trust. It's a dangerous place out there, Elaine. And her friends are like granola bars."

"Granola bars?"

"Yeah. When you take away the sugar and the nuts, all

you have left are the flakes."

Elaine crossed her arms and didn't respond.

"I do have one idea," Eric continued.

"What?"

"I could put her on the phone," Eric said.

"On the phone? Doing what?"

"Selling speaking dates. We can always use the money," Eric said, his mind drifting to the golf course.

"We have plenty of money, Eric. Besides, you agreed you were off the road."

"I know, but I think it would be good for her, give her sales experience and something to sink her teeth into. I've never wanted to push her, but this might be exactly what she needs."

"And you'd do the speeches?" Elaine asked.

"Yeah, of course."

"How many are we talking about?"

"I don't know, a handful. Five or ten, maybe, depending on how well she does."

"Okay," Elaine said with an exasperated breath. "But then that's it, agreed?"

"Yes, I promise."

Chapter Four

SALES IS SLEAZY

Cassidy climbed out of bed and shuffled down the hallway to the kitchen. The celebration the night before had left her in a brain fog, and strong coffee was in order. Her friends were able to party until dawn and make it through the day unscathed, but not her. Three glasses of champagne and a piece of cheesecake had knocked her out.

When Cassidy got to the kitchen, she found a *Go for No!* coffee mug next to the coffee maker and a note that read: *Come see me, I have good news! -Dad.*

Cassidy found her dad behind the desk in his office and plopped down in the chair across from him. "So, what's this good news?"

Eric closed his laptop and looked up. "I have a plan to put you to work."

Cassidy sat up straight and looked at her father. "Wow, great! Doing what?"

"Effective today, you're in sales."

"Sales? Selling what?"

"Me. Selling keynote speeches and workshops."

"I thought you were retired."

"So did I," Eric said. "But this is a good plan. It will give you great work experience."

"What about mom? She seemed adamant that you get off the road."

"We both agreed that a few more speeches aren't a big deal."

"Okay, but sales? That's really not something I'm interested in."

"You don't seem interested in much of anything, Cass."

"Yeah, I know. But sales? Really?"

"What's the problem?"

"Selling stuff is so... *sleazy.*"

"Selling isn't sleazy, Cassidy," Eric said. "Some people go about it in a sleazy way, but the job of selling is an important one. Selling makes the world go round. Nothing happens until someone sells something. This desk, that lamp, your coffee mug, that phone you're glued to—every great idea, every invention, innovation, they all had to be sold."

"I know, but I really don't like pushing stuff on people."

"Is that what you think I teach? How to push stuff on people?"

Cassidy held up her coffee mug and said, "Isn't this pushing stuff on people? Teaching them to 'go for no'?"

"Interesting," Eric said, leaning back in his chair. "That's what you think 'going for no' means?"

"Well, doesn't it?"

"'Going for no' is about persistence, Cass, but more than that—it's about embracing rejection and seeing 'no' as a necessary part of your journey to a 'yes.' Have you read the book?" Eric smirked.

"Yep, you read it to me when I was five. And six. And seven..."

"Let me ask you this," Eric said. "Remember the fundraiser you helped your mother with last year?"

Cassidy nodded. "Yeah, for the animal charity."

"Exactly," Eric said. "How do you think the people who gave all that money ended up at that event? It was because your mother *sold* them on being there."

"Yeah, but charities are different," Cassidy said.

"No, they aren't. Asking is asking. Selling is selling no matter the product or service. We experience rejection as a byproduct of helping someone make a decision. And contrary to what you might think, 'no' is a perfectly acceptable answer."

"So, it's not about wearing people down?"

"Listen, I can see you're afraid of looking pushy. I felt that way, too. But when you have a 'to sell is to serve' attitude, you're not manipulating or trying to trick anyone. You're staying in the game long enough for them to see the value of what you're offering. And if you get good at it, you're not just helping people, you're driving the whole system forward. Businesses grow, economies thrive, and people get paid a lot of money to make that happen."

"Isn't that just justifying it?"

"Well, let me ask you something. Do you like your iPhone?"

"Yeah, of course," Cassidy responded.

"Do your friends like theirs?" Eric asked.

"Obviously."

"Well, Steve Jobs, the guy who brought it into the world,

became a billionaire in part because of that phone. Did he deserve his wealth?"

"I guess. I mean, he created something everyone uses."

"Yes, and more than that, he changed how the world communicates and how people live. It wasn't only about making money, it was about creating something of incredible value that people are willing to pay a lot for because it improves their lives."

Cassidy nodded.

"I've made a lot of money teaching people to reprogram how they feel about failure and rejection, and I want the same for you."

Cassidy stood up, signaling she'd had enough of the lecture, and said, "Dad, I get it."

"And by the way, every 'yes' you've ever gotten required you to have the courage to fail. The willingness to hear 'no.' You sell every day, Cass. You just don't realize it."

Cassidy turned back in the doorway and gave her dad a dutiful smile. "Dad, I love you. This TED Talk is over."

"You never have to feel bad about how I earn a living, either. Every dollar I've ever made, I did it honestly, and I don't apologize for any of it." Eric waved his arms around the room.

"Okay, okay. I'll try to explain that to my friends when they find out I'm in sales and say something snarky about it."

"Or you could just show them your iPhone and ask if they'd like to live without theirs."

"Yeah, that'll go over well."

Chapter Five

CASSIDY DIGS IN

Cassidy sat at the desk in the corner of her room, scrolling through an enormous electronic directory of meeting planners, having no idea where to start. She wasn't psychic, so there was no way to tell which prospects would likely say yes. What was she supposed to do? Call everyone?

Her father had set the goal for her to collect 20 nos every day. One hundred total for the week.

Fun.

Cassidy decided to start by focusing on the industries her father had spoken to most: real estate, insurance, auto dealers, financial planners, SaaS companies and a handful of others.

Three hours and 35 phone calls later, Cassidy had yet to get her first no. She reached a few assistants who offered to take a message, and she left a bunch of voicemails asking people to call her back. No one had. "Going for no" was harder than it looked. Getting 20 nos for the day sounded easy, but now it seemed impossible.

Cassidy glanced at the time and saw it was almost noon.

Time for lunch.

* * *

"Hey, there you are," Elaine said as Cassidy drifted into the kitchen. "I'm making ham and cheese sandwiches. Are you hungry?"

"Not really," Cassidy replied.

"My daughter isn't hungry? What's wrong?"

"Nothing's wrong, Mom," Cassidy said. "I just don't have much of an appetite."

"Come here, sit." Cassidy settled into a seat at the island counter and hung her head, then started to cry. "Cassidy! What's going on with you?"

Cassidy pulled a tissue from a box on the counter and dabbed at her eyes. Finally, she said, "It's this job. I have no idea what I'm doing."

"Hey, you're the one who wanted to work for your father," Elaine said.

"I know, I know, but I can't get past the feeling that I'm bothering people, that I'm an interruption. People have better things to do than listen to my sales pitch."

"Did Dad give you any sales training?"

"No, not really. He gave me a directory and said, 'Go get 'em, Tiger.'"

"That's it?"

"Pretty much."

Elaine shook her head and said, "One of your father's strengths is that he's a sales natural, though I can assure you he didn't start that way. He may have forgotten just how hard it can be, especially when you're new."

"Well, I can't even get anyone to answer the phone, so all I do is leave messages. And the worst thing is, I'm kind of relieved when all I get is voicemail. I'm not sure what I'd do if someone finally answered."

"Listen, I felt the same way when I started in sales. It's

normal. Have you talked to your father? Have you told him how you're struggling?"

"Oh, God, no."

"Well, you're going to have to talk to him sometime. He's going to ask you how it's going, so you might as well face it head-on."

Chapter Six

LET'S MAKE SOME CALLS

Eric was in the family room, watching ESPN, when Cassidy walked in carrying plates with sandwiches and chips. "Hey, there you are," Eric said. "How's it going?"

Cassidy handed her father a plate and sat down next to him on the couch. "Honestly, not great."

"What's happening?"

"Well, in a nutshell, I suck at sales."

Eric laughed. "Wow. You've been selling for what, half a day? You think that's long enough for someone to know if they're good at something?"

"It's long enough to know I don't want to do it."

Eric nodded and said, "I didn't really give you any training, did I? What do you say we eat, then go to my office and make some calls together?"

* * *

Eric pulled an old, tattered directory from the drawer and put it on the desk.

"What's that?" Cassidy asked.

"You've never seen the 'Yellow Pages' before?"

"I've heard of it. I just didn't know people still owned one."

"Yeah, well, I'm old school," said Eric, opening the book

to the “Real Estate” section. “Okay, here’s a company I’ve never worked with. Let’s give them a call.”

Eric picked up the phone on his desk, dialed and hit the speakerphone button. After three rings, the call went to voicemail. To Cassidy’s surprise, Eric hung up the phone.

“Wait, aren’t you going to leave a message?”

“No, that will only slow us down. Most people delete them without even listening. It’s more effective to just move on to the next call, it increases your chances of reaching someone.”

“That would have been good information to know four hours ago,” Cassidy said.

“Sorry,” Eric said sheepishly. “Okay, here’s another company.”

Seven dials later, someone finally answered. “Hello, this is John Thompson,” a man’s voice said.

“John, my name is Eric Bratton. I’m the author of a book called ‘Go for No!’ and I’m calling to find out if your company holds an annual sales meeting?”

“Yes, we do.”

“Great,” Eric said, quickly asking a second question: “Do you bring in professional speakers from outside the company?”

“Well, sometimes, but—”

“One last question,” Eric quickly interjected. “If I send you a copy of my book and you like what I teach, do you have $25,000 in your budget to bring me in?”

“$25,000? Uh, no. We’ve never spent more than

$10,000 for a speaker."

"Oh, okay, I appreciate your time, John," Eric said. "Have a great day!"

Cassidy watched as Eric hung up the phone and returned to scanning the page of company listings.

"Wait, wait! What was that?" Cassidy said, throwing up her hands.

"What was what?"

"That conversation you just had with that guy. You didn't even tell him about 'Go for No!' and you cut him off like three times. It was bizarre, Dad. And you were so rude!"

"Rude? I wasn't rude at all. What I did was respect his time and make good use of my time. If I'd forced him to listen to a sales pitch, only to find out 10 minutes later that my speaking fee was more than he was willing to spend, now *that* would be rude."

"I can't imagine what he's thinking of you right now," Cassidy murmured.

"He's not thinking of me, he's thinking about himself. That conversation is over. He's moved on, trust me."

Cassidy let what her father had just said sink in. "I thought sales was convincing people to buy what you're selling, and you didn't even try."

"Selling isn't about convincing people who don't want what you have to say yes, Cassidy," Eric said. "Selling is about eliminating non-buyers as fast as possible, so you can move on and find people who already want what you've got. Great salespeople spend more time qualifying than they do pitching."

Cassidy shook her head and said, "I don't think I can do this."

"Then don't be you," Eric said.

"Don't be me?" Cassidy repeated, confused. "What do you mean, don't be me?"

"Your problem is that you've already decided you can't sell, Cass. You've defined yourself based on your current limitations rather than your future potential. So, don't be you, Cass—be someone who *can.*"

"That makes no sense," Cassidy said. "People can't just decide to be a different person."

"Really? Why not?" Eric said. "What is movie making all about? It's about projecting an image on a screen and telling a story other people will believe. Right? There's a universe where you don't feel the way you do, a universe where you are someone else, a world where you are unstoppable."

"I'm not sure if I believe that."

"Trust me, Cassidy, it's true. Whether you believe it or not, it's true."

"So, let me get this straight. Your advice is for me to start lying to myself?"

"No, I want you to *stop* lying to yourself because that's what you're doing now. Whenever you tell yourself you're not good enough, that's the lie. Every time you tell yourself how scared you are—and how incapable you feel—it's self-defeating. I'm saying you should act *'as if'* you're already the person you aspire to become, even if you aren't there yet. When you act 'as if,' you train your brain to align with your future, not your present reality. Convince your mind that you're capable, then you'll become capable. But if you keep telling yourself you suck, well, don't be surprised when that becomes a reality you can't seem to escape from."

Cassidy remained silent.

"Okay, let's make some more dials," Eric said and went back to the phone.

Cassidy watched for the next two hours as her father repeated the process of quickly disqualifying non-buyers and presenting only to prospects who were interested.

Finally, to Cassidy's amazement, a sale was made. She watched as her father leaned forward, listening intently to the prospect on the other end of the call. Eric responded by outlining the struggles most companies faced when hiring him, then asked if they were experiencing the same challenges. When the conversation stretched past 10 minutes, Cassidy could tell something had shifted. The initial hesitancy in the prospect's voice had melted into curiosity, then into excitement.

"I'll have my assistant, Cassidy, send over a proposal and the contract. Once we get your deposit, we'll lock in the date and get everything set up. Sound good?"

"Sounds great," the prospect replied. "I'm looking forward to this."

Eric hung up and turned to Cassidy with a grin. "That's all there is to it, Cass. You have conversations with people. Go for no. It's that easy."

Cassidy stood and left the office more depressed than when she arrived. Despite his encouragement, she didn't believe she could do what she just watched her father do.

Chapter Seven

THE GHOST OF CASSIDY FUTURE

Cassidy heard a noise and looked across the room. Someone was lurking in the dark. "Who are you?" Cassidy asked, her heart beating out of her chest. The dark figure stepped forward, and she saw who it was.

She was looking at herself.

"Come, I want to show you something," the figure whispered, motioning for Cassidy to follow her.

Cassidy slowly got up and followed herself across the bedroom toward the wall. "The wall isn't real, Cass. Nothing here is real."

Cassidy stepped forward toward the wall and passed through it as if she was a ghost.

Cassidy found herself in a room she was unfamiliar with. There was an old woman sitting in a chair, gazing out a window, her back to Cassidy. Suddenly the woman turned, and Cassidy saw the woman's face, an empty and hollow look in her eyes.

"Who are you?" Cassidy asked.

"I'm the person you don't want to become."

* * *

Cassidy startled awake and bolted upright, feeling shaken. She looked around the room and saw that she was at home, in her bedroom. She looked at her phone. It was 3:30 in the morning.

Cassidy decided to get up and went to the kitchen. She poured herself a bowl of cereal, got some milk from the refrigerator, and sat down at the kitchen island.

What did the dream mean? Cassidy wondered. It had to mean something, right? Intuitively, she knew the old woman was a future version of herself. The woman clearly wasn't happy. She was resentful. Filled with bitterness and self-doubt.

Her father had challenged her to be someone else. Someone strong. Someone capable. It wouldn't be as easy as he made it out to be, but Cassidy refused to let her future be defined by fear and regret.

What if she stopped thinking of herself as someone who *couldn't* and started thinking of herself as someone who *could*? What kind of future would she have then?

* * *

Cassidy stood in the library doorway, the air smelling of old leather and dust.

Her father loved books, especially first editions of the greatest works in personal development. What had started as a casual hobby had become a passion, fueled by his belief that these books held timeless wisdom.

The collection had grown over the years, filling shelf after shelf in his study. Her dad wasn't just a collector, he was a student of these books. He'd spent countless nights reading and re-reading them, underlining passages. They had shaped the man he had become—resilient, focused, always striving to be better. Now, it was Cassidy's turn to shape herself into the person *she* could be.

She felt that somewhere on these shelves was what she needed to learn to stop feeling stuck and afraid of failure and to start becoming a better self.

The first book Cassidy came across was "Think and Grow Rich," written by Napoleon Hill in 1937. Next to it was "The Science of Getting Rich" by Wallace D. Wattles, written in 1910, and "Acres of Diamonds" by Russell H. Conwell, published in 1890. Each title seemed older than the last.

While Cassidy knew the lessons were timeless, she wanted something more recent. The books weren't just old to her, most of them were written before her father was even born.

An idea flashed across her mind: She'd just go to the bookstore at the mall.

Chapter Eight

STRAWBERRY CREEK UP FOR AUCTION

Eric was pleased with the sales training session he'd had with Cassidy, having no idea how she'd react.

He remembered how crazy the concept of "go for no" seemed at first. He didn't want to hear "no" more often—he wanted what everybody wanted—he wanted to "get to 'yes!'" His desire to avoid failure and rejection had taken time to overcome. It had also taken real effort to overcome some internal barriers he'd once faced around rejection, too.

Eric knew he needed to be patient. Cassidy may have heard "go for no" her whole life, but that didn't mean she was ready for that mindset shift. She needed more time to find her own style, *her* way of "going for no," not his. He made a mental note to do more coaching. Maybe a golf outing was in order. Cassidy could relax a bit, and they could connect. Perhaps he could explain things a bit better.

Eric turned on his laptop to check his email before calling it a day, wading through the regular sea of spam. But then he saw the subject line, which read:

The Partnership Owners of Strawberry Creek Announce Plans to Sell.

Eric's mind raced.

It was finally happening.

After years of emails and phone calls, the dream was within reach. Eric took a deep breath, steadied himself, and dialed the number of the man who ran the ownership group.

"Tom? It's Eric," he said, trying to sound more casual than he felt.

"Hey, buddy, good to hear from you," Tom replied, his tone polite but guarded. "Let me guess—you're calling about the course."

"You got it," Eric said, leaning forward, his voice gaining intensity. "What's the asking price? What's it going to take to make this happen?"

There was a pause on the other end, and Eric could hear the faint rustle of papers. "You mean the *reserve* price?" Tom asked, almost hesitantly.

Eric frowned. "Reserve price? Please tell me you're not putting the course up for auction."

"Yeah," Tom sighed. "That's exactly what I'm telling you."

"You can't do that, Tom! We've been talking about this for years."

"Believe me, I know how much you want it," Tom said, his voice softening. "If it were up to me, I'd sell it to you without a second thought. But I'm just one of the partners. They think they'll get more interest and a higher price if they put it up for auction."

Eric closed his eyes, running a hand over his face, trying to keep his emotions in check. "Tom, you know as well as I do that this course needs work—lots of it. An auction is going to attract speculators who don't care about its history, and what it could be. You know I'm the right buyer. I'm ready to make a fair offer, one that makes sense for everyone."

"I get it, but my hands are tied. The partners outvoted me

and think an auction is the safest way to get the most money. There's nothing I can do."

Eric's grip tightened on the phone. "What's the reserve, then? I need to know what I'm dealing with here."

Tom hesitated again, then said, "The bidding will start at fifteen million."

"Fifteen million?" Eric's voice dropped. "Are you kidding me?"

"It's not the course, it's the land, Eric," Tom said. "There are developers who want to turn the whole area into condos. They see an opportunity to cash out big, and they're probably right."

"What if I make a preemptive offer?" Eric asked. "Something that beats the auction. I'm willing to increase my offer—whatever it takes to stop this insanity."

"If you want to submit a preemptive offer, I'll bring it to the partners, but I can't guarantee they'll consider it. They've set their sights on the auction."

Eric remained silent.

"For what it's worth, I hope you get it, Eric. I really do."

Eric hung up. He had waited too long and heard "no" too many times to back down now.

Chapter Nine

SELF-IMPOSED LIMITATIONS

It was mid-afternoon, and Cassidy sat on a barstool at the kitchen island, surrounded by the stack of books she'd bought. One book gave her an exercise to make a list of self-imposed limitations she thought were holding her back from being successful at selling.

The list she made had 19 items on it.

Yikes.

One of the books was by a guy named Jim Rohn. She'd never heard of him but found his concepts intriguing. Apparently, he was one of Tony Robbins' mentors, so he must know his stuff.

Rohn said that success usually comes down to a half-dozen things. He believed success wasn't complicated or mysterious. All that was required was practicing a handful of fundamental disciplines consistently.

A half-dozen things, huh? Based on this, Cassidy decided to limit her list to just six things.

* * *

The first of the six was obvious: her fear of rejection. But one of the books made a good point Cassidy had never considered. It wasn't being rejected that bothered her, it was what she believed rejection *meant* about *her*.

If someone rejected her offer, it meant they had rejected her. It meant she was somehow unworthy. If someone rejected her offer, it meant she wasn't *good enough*. Cassidy believed rejection was personal. It was hard for her to accept that it wasn't.

Then there was the idea that salespeople were despised, that everyone hates being sold. That selling, by its very nature, was the art of manipulating people. Cassidy knew there was a part of her that felt this way, too. This became the second limiting belief on her list.

Her father had done his best to convince her this wasn't true. People could *use* techniques to manipulate buyers, but the process of selling was just a process. Selling the right product to the right person at the right time at a fair price was to *serve* them.

Cassidy decided she could accept this.

* * *

The third issue was her desire to be perfect. More accurately, her need to be perfect, even though her logical side knew perfection in anything was unattainable.

One of the reasons Cassidy hesitated to approach someone was due to her desire to know everything—to have an answer to every question that could be thrown at her. She was terrified of being "found out." Like the villains in "Scooby Doo." Unmasked as a fraud.

She realized how ridiculous this was. How could she ever know every question someone might ask? It was impossible. If she waited until she was perfect, she'd never get started.

Cassidy had to admit she compared herself to others. If she was being honest, it was why she hadn't stuck with golf. Several new team members were exceptional players, and she couldn't handle being fourth or fifth in the team rankings, so she gave up entirely.

* * *

The fourth item was that she was too young to be taken seriously. "Who does this young girl think she is?" she imagined people saying behind her back.

One of the books pointed out that Mozart began composing music at age 5. Joan of Arc became a military leader at 17. Mark Zuckerberg was 19 when he started Facebook. Bill Gates was only 20 when he founded Microsoft.

The idea that she was too young was only in her head, just like if someone thought they were too old.

* * *

The fifth item on Cassidy's list was something she'd never really considered, but deep down she knew it was true: She had a fear of success.

The phenomenon wasn't a theory, it was real. Despite consciously wanting success, people subconsciously sabotage themselves. They believe success brings greater pressure and higher expectations. Cassidy knew this described her. If she succeeded at selling, maybe her father would expect her to live up to even higher standards. What then?

Some people would say she had "daddy issues." Cassidy knew that wasn't true. She had *Cassidy* issues. Her parents never pressured her to reach unrealistic standards. Wherever her fear of success came from, it wasn't from them.

* * *

The sixth and final item on Cassidy's list was something a little odd. There was a part of her that believed people who made a lot of money were greedy.

Cassidy knew this wasn't true of *all* wealthy people; some, but not all. And it certainly wasn't true about her parents. Her mother and father were extremely generous, both with time and money.

Many professors at school, and most of her friends, had a negative view of rich people. They were against "capitalism," which was funny because they were all well off, wealthy even. Still, they presented capitalism as the root cause of poverty, environmental destruction, and corporate greed—a system that prioritized profit over people.

And it didn't help that virtually every movie portrayed rich people as greedy or evil—it was a trope repeated over and over.

Yet, Cassidy realized making money also provides the opportunity to bring value to the world and make life better for others.

As if on cue, her father appeared in the doorway. "Come on, Cass, we're going to play a round. Meet me out front in five minutes."

Chapter Ten

A CHANGE IN PLANS

With Cassidy in the passenger seat, Eric pulled the car into an almost empty parking lot at the Strawberry Creek Golf Course.

Cassidy was a good golfer, playing on the women's team at USC during her freshman and sophomore years, with a respectable 4-handicap. It was something she had shared with her father growing up, and playing at the collegiate level was a dream realized. But by the end of her sophomore year, the pressure of balancing academics and sports weighed on her, so she decided she had to step away from the team. At least, that was the story she told.

"When's the last time you and I played together here?" Eric asked.

"Here, at Strawberry Creek? I don't know, maybe two years ago."

"Well, you're going to be a little disappointed in the shape of the place."

Once upon a time, Strawberry Creek was a gem. Now, it was falling apart. The once-pristine fairways were overgrown with weeds and uneven patches of grass. The sand traps were unkempt, their edges crumbling and blending into the rough. Cart paths were cracked. The clubhouse windows were grimy and weathered, the paint peeled off its once-polished façade.

Once they'd reached the first tee, Cassidy looked around. "Yeah, I see what you mean. It looks like something out of a zombie apocalypse movie," she said, bending down to fix a divot.

"I know. That's why I'm going to buy it," Eric said, teeing up.

"Buy what?"

"The course," Eric said. "They're putting it up for auction, and I'm going to win it. It means too much to me to just sit by and watch. I'm going to save this place."

"Seems a little crazy. Does Mom know about this?"

"Not yet," Eric said. "You know, it was here at Strawberry Creek 25 years ago that I lost my balance and hit my head on the rocks and—"

"In your dream, you mean," Cassidy interrupted.

Eric didn't reply.

"Wow, I don't know what to say," Cassidy said.

"I'd like you to say you're in," Eric said. "I don't need you to sell speaking dates, I won't have the time to deliver them. I need you to sell corporate memberships and sign-up sponsors."

Cassidy went silent as they walked up the fairway. If she couldn't sell her own father's speaking engagements, how could she sell this? She shook her head, trying to will the thought away.

"By the way, what were you working on back at the house?" Eric asked.

"Oh, nothing really. I was making a list of all my self-limiting beliefs. I don't understand how I got them, and I really don't know how I'm ever going to get rid of them."

"Have I ever told you about the drops of dye concept?"

"I feel another TED Talk coming on."

Eric ignored her. "Picture your mind as a fishbowl full of water. Now, imagine putting in drops of yellow dye, which are all the limiting thoughts and beliefs that have gone into your mind over time. If you wanted to get rid of the yellow dye, you'd just empty the fishbowl and refill it with clear water, right? The problem is the brain doesn't work that way. There is no way to dump the yellow water. The thoughts that have gone into your mind over the last 20 years will be there forever."

"I'm stuck with my limiting beliefs?" Cassidy said. "That's real motivating, Dad."

"I didn't say there's nothing you can do about them," Eric said. "The answer is to add different thoughts—uplifting and supportive thoughts—made of blue dye into the water. Then, what would happen?"

"It would turn green."

"Yes, and that's how it works with thoughts. Don't waste your time trying to get rid of the old ones. Just add so many better, empowering thoughts that you literally override and recolor your water."

Cassidy went silent as her father putt the ball and watched it drop into the cup. Finally, she said: "When's the auction?"

"Friday," Eric said.

"Okay, I'm coming with you."

Chapter Eleven
THE BIDDING STARTS

The room was buzzing with low chatter, and a palpable sense of anticipation filled the air. Cassidy stood beside her father at the back of the auction room packed with bidders and curious onlookers. All eyes were fixed on the podium where the auctioneer adjusted his glasses, about to begin.

A camera crew from a local San Diego TV station hovered in the corner, the lens zooming in on bidders as the auctioneer spoke into the microphone.

"Ladies, gentlemen, let's begin the auction for Strawberry Creek Golf Course. We'll start the bidding at fifteen million."

Cassidy glanced at her dad, his face a steely look of determination she'd seen many times before. A hand shot up across the room—$15 million. Eric raised his paddle casually—$16 million.

When the bidding reached $20 million, Cassidy started to feel anxious and queasy. Then it went to 25. Then 27.

Finally, the bids began to slow. Suddenly, a man in the second row called out, "Thirty million!"

Cassidy's heart skipped a beat. They had agreed under no circumstances would they bid over 30. It was over. They'd lost.

The auctioneer's hammer hovered above the block. "Do I hear thirty-one? Thirty-one? Thirty-one going once, going twice—"

Eric raised his paddle.

"We've got thirty-one million!" the auctioneer declared. Cassidy's eyes widened, and her mouth hung open. For a moment, no one moved until a figure at the front of the room called out, "Thirty-two million."

Cassidy relaxed. They were off the hook. Then, her father lifted his paddle. "Thirty-two and a half million."

Cassidy's breath caught in her throat as the room went silent, every eye looking in their direction. "Oh, God, Dad, what are you doing?"

Eric did not respond.

The auctioneer raised his gavel, scanning the room. "Going once... going twice..."

Cassidy could hear her own heartbeat as she waited for the final strike. With a sharp crack of the gavel, the auctioneer's voice rang out, "Sold! To Mr. Eric Bratton for thirty-two and a half million dollars!"

The room exploded with applause.

The camera crew zoomed in, capturing the victorious moment as Eric shook hands with the auctioneer, sealing the deal. Cassidy felt a combination of fear and pride surge through her. Her father had done what he said he would do, but was it the right decision?

Chapter Twelve

ELAINE BLOWS A FUSE

Eric and Cassidy stepped through the front door of the house and stopped dead in their tracks. Elaine stood in the center of the living room, her arms crossed over her chest, eyes flashing.

"You bought a golf course?"

"Not just any golf course, Elaine, it's Strawberry Creek and—"

"That's not the point," she snapped, unfolding her arms and throwing them in the air. "I don't care if you bought Augusta National. You spent thirty-two million dollars of our money without even asking me. I had to find out on television!"

Eric sighed and rubbed the back of his neck. "I was going to tell you, but everything happened so fast."

"I did the math, Eric, and there's no way we can come up with that kind of money. Even if we drained our savings and our 401k's, we've got nowhere near that amount."

Cassidy shifted uncomfortably from foot to foot, unsure whether she should stay or slip away. She had seen her parents argue before, but this was different.

Eric stepped forward with his hands raised in a calming gesture. "I know it's a lot to take in, but this wasn't a rash decision. Strawberry Creek means something to us. It's an investment. Cassidy and I are going to turn it around and bring it back to its former glory. You know I've been thinking about this for years."

Elaine shook her head and looked toward Cassidy. "And you, you've been in on this for how long?"

Cassidy felt a sting of guilt. At the auction, wrapped up in the moment, she hadn't even considered how her mother might react. "Well, I—"

"Never mind," Elaine said, cutting her off.

Elaine turned her gaze back to Eric. "You've gambled everything we have on a pipe dream. And don't forget, at least half of what we own is from the sale of the art galleries, money I worked my ass off to earn."

Eric's jaw tightened, but his voice stayed calm. "It's not a gamble. It's a calculated risk. I've reviewed the numbers, and we can make this work." Eric stepped closer. "I didn't mean to blindside you. I should have told you and, for that, I'm sorry. But I know we can make this a success. We have the resources, the connections, and the vision. Strawberry Creek is more than a golf course; it's part of our history. We're supposed to own it. I'm sure of it."

* * *

Elaine stood in the doorway of Eric's office, her arms crossed. "Why didn't you tell me?" she asked softly.

Eric looked up from his laptop and leaned back in his chair, struggling to find the words. "I wasn't trying to keep it from you. I just—"

"Come on, Eric, we've been married a long time—of course you were hiding it from me. The question is, why?"

"I don't know. I guess I was afraid that maybe you'd think I was having a midlife crisis."

“Are you?”

Eric shook his head. “No, Elaine. This course isn’t an emotional reaction to getting older. It’s a dream I’ve had for a long time… one I can’t let go of.”

“I understand, but why didn’t you tell me?”

“I was afraid you’d say no.”

Elaine remained quiet for a bit, then said, “Are you afraid the course will fail?”

Eric nodded.

Elaine reached out and took his hand. “You, afraid of failure? That doesn’t sound like you. You’re the guy who teaches everyone the key to success is to fail more often.”

“I know. Maybe I’ve gotten complacent. Too comfortable. I forgot what it feels like to go for something big, and I’m more scared than I want to admit.”

“Listen, if it fails, it fails,” Elaine said. “And if it does, we’ll figure it out together, just like we always have. I’ve gotten a bit too comfortable, too. Maybe it’s time for us both to be willing to take a few more risks.”

Chapter Thirteen
COMING TO GRIPS WITH REALITY

With the excitement of the auction behind him, Eric began the process of hiring a consulting company to help with the planning and logistics. The terms of the auction required him to put down a 20% deposit within three days, which he had done. The balance was due within 30 days. He'd forfeit the deposit if he could not come up with the money.

He needed to get in gear.

Eric decided to start with the National Golf Course Owners Association, which offered resources, including a directory of consultants. Deep in thought and mindlessly scrolling through his emails, he stopped on a LinkedIn notification of a message that read:

> *I saw that you purchased the Strawberry Creek golf course. I have something of great importance to discuss with you. - Reena Chaudry*

It didn't give off the typical scam vibes. Eric clicked on her profile. Her name appeared to be of Indian or Pakistani descent. He could not remember ever meeting her. Her profile was sparse. No photo. The company name was listed as Chaudry & Associates for the last decade and not much else. It could be a scam, but Eric's curiosity got the best of him. He sent a direct message with his phone number. Minutes later, his cell phone rang.

"This is Eric Bratton."

"Thank you for responding," Reena replied.

"Do we know each other?" Eric asked.

"That is an interesting question," Reena said. "In a way, yes, we know each other."

"Listen, I'm swamped. You mentioned Strawberry Creek. What do you want? What's the offer?"

"Oh, I'm not selling you anything, Mr. Batton," Reena chuckled. "I wish it were that simple. Okay, here goes. Did anything strange happen to you twenty-five years ago?"

"What makes you ask that?" Eric said, his grip tightening around the phone.

After a brief pause, Reena said: "This is going to sound a bit strange, but I have had dreams that started suddenly twenty-five years ago, dreams that involve you."

Eric felt a cold prickle down his spine. "Me?"

"In the dreams, I work as a maid in a large house on the edge of a golf course."

Eric remained silent.

"The thing is, these dreams feel incredibly real—almost as if they are memories of something that actually happened. In them, I work for a man and his wife. The man is an author, his wife runs an art gallery."

Eric's heartbeat quickened.

"The man I work for is you, Mr. Bratton," Reena said. "I didn't know it was you until I saw you on TV at the auction, but the man in the dreams *is* you. There's no question about it."

Eric's throat went dry. Twenty-five years ago? None of this made sense. "Look," he said, his voice sharper than intended, "if this is some kind of scam, you can—"

"It's not a scam," Reena interrupted. "I can't explain it much better than I already have. But if you allow me to talk to you in person, I think I can prove that I'm telling the truth."

"Prove it? How?"

"It's difficult to describe over the phone. But there are things I remember... details about you, your life, the house in the dream. Things I couldn't possibly know unless—"

"Unless what?"

"Unless the dreams are more than just dreams," she finished softly.

Eric opened his mouth to refuse, but something stopped him. Her voice wasn't desperate or overly pushy—it carried an odd mix of certainty and honesty. Part of him wanted to hang up, but the part desperate for answers couldn't ignore her.

Chapter Fourteen
REENA'S DREAMS

Reena Chaudry gripped the steering wheel as the tires crunched over the gravel driveway leading up to the Bratton house. It was an impressive estate, tucked away from the noise of the city, with manicured lawns stretching out like a green ocean. The mid-morning sun cast shadows through the old oak trees lining the drive.

Reena parked and made her way to the door, raised her hand, and knocked. She waited, then heard muffled footsteps approaching from within. The door swung open, and there he was: Eric James Bratton. He looked almost exactly as Reena remembered, though he was a bit older now. But it was clearly the same man.

* * *

Eric, Elaine, Cassidy, and Reena sat around the dining room table. "I hate to sound rude, but I've got to start by telling you I don't believe any of this," Elaine said.

"Well, can you explain how I know so many details about your house?" Reena asked.

"You could have gotten floor plans from the city, or from the article about our house in Architectural Digest," Elaine said.

"And my incentive to lie?" Reena asked.

"I don't know, you tell me."

"Okay, okay, let's keep this civil," Eric said.

"I *am* being civil," Elaine said, "but I don't like being

played."

"Cassidy, could you get a pitcher of water and some glasses from the kitchen?" Eric asked.

Cassidy nodded, stood, and headed off.

Everyone sat silently until Cassidy returned with the water and a tray with four glasses.

Reena filled her glass, took a sip, then said: "I understand why you're skeptical, Mrs. Bratton. A stranger shows up at your door, spinning some kind of wild tale. It is unusual."

"Unusual?" Elaine blurted out.

"Mom, please," Cassidy said.

Elaine covered her mouth and nodded an apology.

"Tell us more things you think you know about the house," Eric said. "Things that couldn't possibly be found online or from a magazine article."

"Okay, let's start with the kitchen. There's a drawer under the island, the second drawer from the right. It doesn't close all the way unless you jiggle it slightly. It catches on a little notch at the back. And inside that drawer, tucked at the very back, is a small brass key."

Cassidy stood again. "Hang on, I'll be right back." Everyone waited for Cassidy to return, and when she did, she had a brass key in her hand. "It was right where she said."

Reena pressed forward. "That key is for a padlocked wooden chest hidden in the attic. The chest has nothing of value in it, just some old letters, dried flowers, and a tiny pewter figure of a horse."

Elaine's mouth opened, but no words came out. Finally, Elaine said: "There was a wooden chest in the attic when we moved in. I tried to open it, but there was no key. I had to use a screwdriver to pry it open."

"What was in the box?" Eric asked.

"A few old letters, some dried flowers, and a tiny metal horse."

* * *

Reena turned her attention to Eric and said, "You have a private study, one you don't show to guests. It's where you keep your personal collection of rare, first-edition books."

Eric's gaze locked on Reena as the color drained slightly from his cheeks. "How could you possibly know that?"

"I've already told you, Mr. Bratton. It's because I've been here before—many, many times."

"In your dreams," Cassidy said, more a statement than a question.

Reena nodded. "Yes. In my dreams. In my dreams, I've scrubbed floors, done laundry, and cooked meals here. The third step from the bottom of the staircase squeaks when you put weight on it. I know that the window in the master bedroom sticks when you try to open it, and there's a faint crack in the glass that you only see when the afternoon sun hits it at just the right angle. Am I correct?"

Elaine's voice was barely a whisper now. "But... why? Why would you have these dreams? Why this house? Why Eric and I?"

"I don't know why," Reena said. "But they've been a part of my life for so long. Now, here's the weirdest part."

"There's a weirder part?" Cassidy asked.

"In my earliest dreams, there were two of you."

"You mean Eric and I?" Elaine said.

"No. Eric and Eric." Reena said.

"Two of me?" Eric said.

"Yes, there are two of you, Mr. Bratton," Reena said. "One is the man I work for, but then, in some dreams, there was also a *look-a-like* twin version."

"An identical twin?" Eric repeated, his pulse quickening.

"In this dream, I'm in the kitchen, and the twin appears. I was so surprised—"

"—you dropped a blue ceramic platter," Eric said, finishing the sentence. "You didn't expect me to be there so late in the morning. I asked your name, and you said it was Renee."

"Renee is the American version of Reena," Reena said. "You asked about your wife, and I told you she was away on a business trip, buying art."

"Did you ever see these two *versions* of me in the house *together?*" Eric asked.

"Yes. I saw you both several times," Reena said.

"This is bonkers," Cassidy whispered.

"I knew it!" Eric exclaimed. "No one believed me when I said I traveled to the future and met another version of myself. This proves I'm not nuts."

Reena hesitated. "Does it, though?"

Eric's excitement faltered. "What do you mean?"

"I don't know exactly what happened to you back then, but I'm not sure you traveled in time. I didn't," Reena said.

"That you know about," Cassidy added, raising an eyebrow.

"Okay, whatever, let's just say this is true," Elaine said. "What does it all mean?"

"I'm not sure, Mrs. Bratton," Reena said. "I believe I've had these dreams for a reason. And when the universe shows you something, even if you don't fully understand it, it's dangerous to ignore it. And there's one more thing I need to tell you—it might be the key to why I'm here."

"What?" Cassidy and Elaine blurted at the same time.

"I'm the owner of Chaudry & Associates. We design golf courses."

* * *

After Reena dropped her bombshell, Eric asked her to come into his office. If this was why she was here, there was no time to lose.

Reena began. "You've got one big problem," she said after Eric caught her up on his plans. She reviewed the single-page financial statement. "You're going to need more money than you think."

"More? How much more?" Eric asked.

"A minimum of seventy-five million if you want to turn Strawberry Creek into a world-class resort with a hotel and a restaurant," Reena said. "Even if you're willing to put off some items on your list, you might get it done for sixty. In a perfect world, you'd have done market research, a feasibility report, and a profit analysis. Also, you would have determined the market demand for a high-end country club and resort. It appears you skipped all those steps."

"You're telling me I need to double my budget and start from scratch on a business plan," Eric said, exhaling. "Fantastic. Just what I needed."

"I'm not telling you this to discourage you. I'm telling you because I've seen people make the same mistakes, and I don't want that to happen to you. There's a way forward—but it's going to take work—and some help."

Eric studied her face. "And you're offering to help me out of the goodness of your heart?"

Reena smiled. "Not entirely. I believe in this project, but it's more than that. The dreams have been a part of my life for so long. I've always felt there was a reason for them, a purpose I didn't understand... until now."

"What do you mean?"

"I think I'm supposed to help you. And before you ask—no, I don't expect you to pay me for this. Consider it my way of giving back to the universe for finally revealing why I've been dreaming about you and this place."

Eric frowned. "Why would you dedicate so much time and effort to something like this without compensation?"

"Because sometimes," Reena said, "it's not about the money. It's about the story we're living. Yours and mine, too."

Eric was torn between disbelief and excitement. He had never met anyone like Reena before.

"So, what's the catch?"

"The only catch is that you have to be willing to listen. No shortcuts, no skipping the hard stuff. If we're going to do this, we do it right. Deal?"

"Deal."

As their hands clasped, Reena said, "No matter how tough it gets, no matter how many setbacks we face, we don't give up on this. The universe doesn't hand us these opportunities for nothing. You owe it to yourself to see it through."

Eric nodded. For the first time in years, he felt a spark of purpose reignite—a sense that he wasn't just chasing a dream but fulfilling a destiny.

Chapter Fifteen

CASSIDY GETS BUSY SELLING

While her father and Reena worked on drawing up business and architectural plans for the course, Cassidy dove head-first into the task of selling sponsorships and corporate memberships.

It didn't go well.

Cassidy called every upscale car dealership within 250 miles. No luck. She moved on to high-end hotels but, again, nothing. It was the same with PR agencies, CPAs, law firms, financial institutions, insurance companies, and every other category she could think of.

No, no, no, no, no.

The two most common objections were tight budgets and long-standing relationships with other golf courses. But the biggest problem was that Strawberry Creek had become shabby and neglected, something no one wanted to be associated with.

Cassidy stood up from the small desk she was working at in her bedroom and stretched. Time for a snack.

Speaking of snacks, Cassidy knew she needed to get to the gym. She was so focused on work she was not taking very good care of herself and felt sluggish. It was weird how spending energy working out actually gave you more energy later in the day.

When Cassidy walked into the kitchen, Reena was there. "Tea?" Reena asked, pouring water into a mug.

"No thanks. I need a Red Bull." Cassidy opened the

refrigerator. "I'm exhausted. I feel like I am literally riding on a roller coaster. Someone seems interested, I send information, then I get a bunch of nos. I follow up with the interested person, and they don't call me back—"

"Ah, the yes-no emotional roller coaster," Reena sighed. "Welcome to sales."

"Wait. You sell?" Cassidy asked. "I thought you designed courses?"

"Of course, I sell. To be successful at what I do, I have no choice. No one does. I have to sell myself all the time. I have to sell my competence. I have to sell my vision and my ideas. I sell hard, too. And people tell me 'no' a lot."

Cassidy remembered her conversation with her father about everyone being in sales. "How do you deal with it?" Cassidy asked.

"Have you ever been on an airplane with a little turbulence?" Reena asked.

"Of course," said Cassidy, sipping her drink.

"It's a bit unsettling at first. The plane shaking and buffering against the wind. Eventually, you settle in. You see that it's not going away. In fact, it's keeping the plane in the air. And before long, you hardly notice it."

"Until, bam!" Cassidy said, slapping her hands together.

"True enough," Reena said with a slight grin. "But the longer you do it, the more you'll settle into the turbulence—because it's always a little bumpy no matter how good you are. Now, if you are on a roller coaster, it's up to you to get off of it."

"I'm not sure it's possible," Cassidy said.

"You get off the roller coaster by making the conscious choice," Reena said, pointing to Cassidy's head. "And physically, move. Change your state. Get up. Take a walk. Go to the gym. Listen to your favorite music. Watch some cat videos."

Cassidy smirked at the mention of cat videos. "You think a kitten falling off a table will fix me?"

"No, but it might fix your moment. And moments add up to your life, don't they?" Reena said as she got up from the stool. "And, congratulations, by the way."

"Congratulations, for what?" Cassidy asked.

"For all the nos you've collected," Reena said.

"You read Dad's book, didn't you?"

"Yes," Reena said. "Twenty-five years ago, I sat down with your father's book and read it cover to cover."

"Twenty-five years ago?" Cassidy asked

"Yes," Reena said. "In one of my dreams."

Chapter Sixteen

NEVER THINK ALONE

Cassidy felt much better after the pep talk from Reena the day before. She also took refuge in listening to podcasts to stay motivated and managed to squeeze in a session at the gym. Someone said on one of the shows that you should never think alone.

Cassidy knew she was going around in circles by herself and getting nowhere. She needed advice from people who could see solutions she couldn't. Asking for help wasn't in her DNA, but, like everything else lately, she'd have to learn.

She pulled into the familiar parking lot at USC's Dedeaux Field, the towering palm trees swaying gently in the early afternoon breeze. She was going unannounced to see her old golf coach and pick her brain.

Cassidy parked the car and headed to the golf facility tucked behind the athletic complex. Taking a deep breath, she knocked on the door.

"Come in," she heard a familiar voice say.

Sitting behind a large metal desk sat Coach Barb Reynolds, looking as lean and focused as ever, her salt-and-pepper hair cut short, arms tanned from decades of play in the California sun. Behind her was a bookcase cluttered with trophies, plaques, and team photos, the faint smell of leather golf bags lingering in the air.

"Cassidy!" she said with surprise. "Well, this is a face I didn't expect to see today. What brings you here, my dear?"

"Well, you," Cassidy replied.

"Me?"

Cassidy updated Barb on the situation with the golf course, and she raised an eyebrow, clearly surprised. "Your family owns Strawberry Creek?"

"I know, crazy, right?" Cassidy said nervously.

"I played there a few times over the years," Barb said. "I liked it a lot."

"It's in really rough shape now, but it has potential," Cassidy said. "We're working on a plan to help bring it back to life, but it's a huge project. We think Strawberry Creek can be a world-class golf resort."

Barb leaned back, studying her. "Sounds ambitious. What do you need from me?"

"Well," Cassidy said, hesitating, "I was hoping you might have some advice—maybe some contacts who could help me. I need to bring in investors, sponsors, and the right people to make this dream a reality. To be honest, I'm feeling kind of lost, and we're running out of time."

Barb looked up thoughtfully, then leaned forward and rested her elbows on the desk. "The thing you need is a name—someone with a reputation in the golf world who can get people to take you seriously or the backing of someone who can vouch for your vision."

Cassidy nodded. "I was afraid you'd say that."

"Not easy, is it?"

"No. I am failing. Big time. I'm so frustrated that these people can't see what we see. I got hung up on three times—yesterday!"

Barb grimaced. "Oh, wow, that's rough. Can I remind

you of something?"

"Anything."

Barb smiled. "You don't win by avoiding the sand traps, Cassidy. You win by learning how to get out of them."

* * *

Cassidy's next stop was a meeting with Robert Henley, the executive vice president of the La Costa Golf Resort in Carlsbad.

Cassidy stepped into the elegant lobby, the scent of flowers mingling with freshly brewed coffee drifting from the dining room. The walls were lined with photographs of famous golfers, and the air hummed with quiet, professional energy. She smoothed down her blazer and adjusted her posture as a concierge directed her to Henley's office.

"I'm obviously not here to try and sell you anything," Cassidy began once she was settled in a chair opposite Henley. "You are, technically, a competitor."

"Well, I'm glad to hear that," he chuckled. "To be frank, we don't see Strawberry Creek as a competitor. We've renovated our Champions and Legends Course, making us a top-tier golf destination, and you've yet to start. There really is no comparison between the two, is there?"

Ouch.

"Well, still, I'm glad you agreed to meet with me."

"You'd be surprised how few people have the guts to call and ask. What can I do for you, Cassidy?"

"What can you tell me about the Kia Classic?" Cassidy

asked, quickly changing the subject.

"It's one of the highlights of our calendar. I imagine you're interested in learning how it came together?"

Cassidy nodded.

Henley leaned back in his chair. "Well, the Kia Classic is a beast, that's for sure. We have some of the top female golfers from around the world coming to compete, and that kind of prestige doesn't just happen overnight. It takes careful planning, the right partnerships, and an immense amount of attention to detail."

Henley went on for the next half hour, sharing the details from the course to the food and service.

Cassidy absorbed his words, feeling both excited and daunted by the road ahead. "Thank you so much for your time, Mr. Henley. This has been incredibly helpful."

Henley extended his hand. "I can tell you're serious about this, Cassidy, and that's the most important thing. Let me know if you ever want to see the behind-the-scenes in action. I'd be happy to give you a tour during the next Kia Classic."

"I'd love it," Cassidy said. "I'll definitely take you up on that."

As she shook his hand, Cassidy had a question pop into her head. "One last thing. If you were me, where would you start?"

Henley leaned in as if he were telling her a secret and said, "Honestly, I'd stop going after the small fish like you've been doing and try to land a whale with big money."

"The big money? Who has the big money?"

Henley whispered, “The UAE, for one. There’s a rumor that the power brokers in Dubai are interested in getting into sports, and they want to make a splash.”

Chapter Seventeen

CHASING YASMIN

Cassidy woke at the crack of dawn, made her way to the kitchen to get a cup of coffee, then went outside to fetch the Wall Street Journal from the driveway. Her dad really was old-school, she thought to herself and smiled. She was reading the business section when the headline caught her eye:

"Yasmin Al-Hakim to Receive International Award for Advancing Women's Rights in the UAE."

The article said Al-Hakim had become a symbol of progress for women in the Middle East. The accompanying photo showed a striking woman dressed in elegant attire, standing alongside a group of dignitaries at the United Nations.

"You need to land a whale with big money," Robert Henley had said. *"And there's a rumor the UAE wants to get into sports."*

This was it. This was the opportunity Cassidy had been waiting for. If she could get to Yasmin Al-Hakim, she might be able to explain how an alliance with Strawberry Creek would be a good opportunity for them both. But there was a problem. The banquet was that night.

In New York.

Cassidy calculated the flight time from San Diego to New York City, plus the time change. If she wanted to get there before the banquet was over, she needed to be on a direct flight by noon. It was almost 7 a.m.

There was no time to think.

There was only time to act.

Cassidy went online and booked a 10:30 a.m. flight that arrived at JFK at 7:10 p.m. Luckily, her credit card had enough 'open to buy' for the ticket. Score.

Cassidy packed a bag and left a note: *Gone to New York for a business meeting. Back tomorrow! Love, Cass.*

* * *

The cab pulled up to the Four Seasons at 8:30 p.m., and a valet opened her door. Cassidy hopped out and entered the exquisite lobby, buzzing with chatter from a sea of tuxedos and sparkling gowns. The air filled with the scent of expensive perfume. The question was: Could she talk her way into the banquet? It only took a few minutes to discover the answer was no. Security was tight, and the people who guarded the doors to the ballroom were in no mood to make exceptions. She'd wait.

By the time the banquet ended, Cassidy was exhausted. Suddenly, a ripple of excitement brought her back to life when she saw Yasmin Al-Hakim walking in her direction surrounded by a small entourage.

Cassidy had two thoughts pop into her mind. The first was: *Who do you think you are? This is insane! Don't approach her; you'll only look like a fool.* The second thought was: *You traveled all this way to meet this woman, and there she is, standing right in front of you, and you're going to give up now?*

This is it, Cassidy thought. Shoot your shot. If you miss, so be it, failure is acceptable. But not trying? That was unforgivable. This was a *go for no* moment if ever there was one.

Cassidy took a deep breath, pushed through the crowd and called out: “Ms. Al-Hakim! Ms. Al-Hakim!”

Yasmin paused, her gaze shifting toward Cassidy, and said, “Yes?”

“My name is Cassidy Bratton. I flew here from San Diego specifically to meet you.”

Yasmin’s eyebrows arched, a flicker of surprise and amusement crossing her face. “You flew all the way to New York to speak with me? Whatever for?”

“I want to share an idea I think you’ll really like that could help us both. All I need is a few minutes of your time.”

Yasmin studied Cassidy for a moment, then smiled. “Alright. You have my attention.”

Cassidy and Yasmin found a quiet corner of the lobby, and Cassidy presented her vision for a groundbreaking partnership with the course.

Yasmin listened, her expression thoughtful, and then Cassidy remembered: “Oh, and here’s the business plan,” Cassidy said, handing Yasmin the document her father and Reena had put together. Cassidy gave Yasmin some time to flip through pages, then asked, “Is this something you might be interested in?”

“You give me too much credit, Cassidy. Yes, I am fighting for women’s freedom, and an alliance of this nature is intriguing, but something this grand is above my influence. To make a project as big as this, you will need to present it to Majid Al Futtaim.”

"Who is he?"

"Majid is a multi-billionaire investor. He is the owner of the Dubai Mall, the largest shopping mall in the world, making Dubai a global tourist destination. He also happens to be my brother."

"Oh, wow. Is he here?" Cassidy asked, trying not to sound desperate.

Yasmin chuckled, shaking her head. "Oh, no. If you want to meet with Majid, you'll need to get yourself to Dubai."

"I see..." Cassidy said, her voice trailing off. "Can I schedule a meeting with him?"

"What's wrong with now?" Yasmin asked.

"Like, now, now? I don't have my passport," Cassidy stammered, feeling the opportunity slipping away.

Yasmin leaned closer, her eyes twinkling. "Don't worry. I may not wield as much power as I'd like, but I have enough clout to get you on our plane without one."

A few minutes later, Cassidy found herself in a sleek, black SUV, racing through the streets of Manhattan toward a private airfield. She had barely caught her breath before she was escorted onto a luxurious Gulfstream jet, with polished wood paneling and soft ambient lighting. Her family had money, but this was on another level.

A flight attendant handed her a glass of chilled champagne as she settled into a cream-colored seat, the leather so soft it felt like sinking into a cloud. Then the jet took off with a gentle lurch, and Cassidy watched New York City's skyline recede into the distance.

Chapter Eighteen
ERIC'S BIG NO

Eric wasn't sure what Cassidy was up to, but he couldn't fully leave the course's fate on her shoulders. With that thought, he stepped into the sprawling lobby of Ironwood Capital Partners, a boutique investment firm known for backing bold, unconventional projects.

The meeting room was stark but sophisticated, and the floor-to-ceiling windows offered a panoramic view of San Diego. Rachel Novak, a senior partner, greeted him with a firm handshake. She was sharp, polished, and radiated authority.

"Eric, thanks for coming in," Rachel said, motioning for him to sit. "We've reviewed your proposal. It's interesting."

Eric smiled. "Thank you, Rachel. I truly believe this venture is not just a business opportunity but a chance to redefine what a golf course can be."

Eric launched into his pitch, highlighting the projected ROI for their firm. He painted a picture of rolling greens and elite clientele, a place that would attract both avid golfers and corporations seeking unique retreats. When he finished, Rachel nodded thoughtfully, setting the proposal aside. "It's a compelling vision, Eric. And I can tell you're passionate about it. But passion alone doesn't guarantee success."

Eric stiffened. "I've backed everything I've presented with data. The market—"

Rachel sighed. "I hear you. But golf is a declining sport

in many demographics. Courses are closing faster than they're opening. Even with the sustainability angle, the risk outweighs the reward for us."

Eric's stomach sank. No matter how many nos you hear and how good you get, the physical sensations of rejection will manifest. Eric recognized the feeling well.

"With respect, this isn't just another golf course. It's—"

"It's a dream," she interrupted, her tone softening, "and I admire that. But Ironwood doesn't invest in dreams unless they come with ironclad guarantees. It's too big a gamble, Eric. We've got to pass."

"I've mitigated the risks as much as possible," Eric said his voice steady. He knew better than to argue, it would only make things worse.

Rachel gave him a small, almost apologetic smile. "Eric, I wish you the best of luck. But this isn't a fit for us."

Eric nodded, forced a tight smile, and extended his hand. "Thank you for your time."

Walking out of the building, the weight of rejection pressed down on him. He'd swung for the fences and was proud of that. Still, he thought this was when everything would fall into place, but instead, it felt like everything was falling apart.

For the first time in years, Eric wondered if his belief in persistence had hit its limit.

Chapter Nineteen
THE PRESENTATION

Dubai, the capital and largest city in the UAE, is located on the southeastern coast of the Persian Gulf. With a population of approximately three million people, it's also the political and economic center of the country.

Cassidy was amazed by the city's modern skyline and felt ashamed for thinking the rest of the world was not as developed as America. She clearly needed to get out more.

Cassidy sat in a spacious, opulently decorated room inside Burj Khalifa, the tallest building in the world, awaiting the arrival of Majid. Yasmin Al-Hakim was in a chair in the corner, observing, there merely for support.

Cassidy was on her own.

The night before, Cassidy texted her parents to let them know she was fine and would be gone for an extra day or two, and not to worry. She left out the part about being in Dubai.

She'd barely slept, spending much of the night researching everything she could on Majid's background. The most promising thing was that Majid was a driver of progress who advocated for reforms and empowering women. Cassidy knew that was the angle to take. She would use the Kia Classic at La Costa Resort as an example of what she felt was possible for the advancement of women in golf.

* * *

Majid came in, exchanged pleasantries with Cassidy, and

said, "It's extraordinarily unusual for me to take a meeting like this, but you are here, and I trust Yasmin's judgment. Proceed."

"Thank you for seeing me," Cassidy said, her voice steady despite the fluttering nerves in her chest. She slid the business plan across the table. "I'm excited to share my vision for this course and to discuss how I believe this partnership could be mutually beneficial."

Majid took the business plan from Cassidy but didn't open it. Instead, he asked her: "Who are you?"

"My name is Cassidy Bratton, I'm from San Diego, California, and—"

"I am not asking for your name or where you are from, I know that already," Majid said. "What I'm asking is, at your core, who are *you?* What do you believe in? What moves you? Who does Cassidy Bratton idolize? What is your mission in the world?"

Cassidy swallowed hard, then did her best to provide answers to questions she had never considered. "I'm not sure I have answers to all those questions yet. In fact, to be honest, I've been really lost for a while now, but I'm starting to realize some things."

"There is a proverb that says, *all who wander are not lost*," Majid said with a slight smile. "Continue."

"Well, I do know that I believe in the potential of people, places, and ideas. I've seen how passion and hard work can transform something broken into something beautiful, and that's what drives me. And who do I idolize? I idolize people who have faced failure, adversity, and rejection—people who were told they couldn't do something but proved everyone wrong. I admire people who dare to dream big. People who saw things that didn't exist, yet found a way to make those things real. Those are my heroes."

"And at your core, Cassidy Bratton, who are you?"

"At my core?" Cassidy said slowly, feeling the truth of the words settling over her. "Well, I have been a scared person who spent far too much time worried about what other people think of me, of not measuring up."

"And now?"

"I don't know, except I am sitting here in this incredible office making a proposal to one of the richest and most powerful men in the world. You tell me."

Majid let go with a laugh and looked in Yasmin's direction.

"I told you," Yasmin said.

"My father says the world isn't waiting for us to make up our minds—it's moving, with or without us," Cassidy continued. "I've been trying to figure out where I fit in that movement, and I think I'm starting to understand. I want to be someone who's not afraid to do hard things."

Majid gave a slight nod and opened the business plan. Cassidy sat silently and fidgeted nervously. She was tempted several times to jump in and say more, but she restrained herself.

After what seemed like an eternity, Majid returned his attention back to Cassidy. "I can see that you are passionate and did well to come here and make your case in person. And based on this proposal, it is obvious you have done your homework."

"Thank you, sir," Cassidy said with a sense of relief.

"The problem is your numbers don't add up."

Cassidy's heart sank.

"You are not asking for nearly enough. To do a project of this size and do it the right way would require double what you're asking for, perhaps more."

Cassidy's breath caught. Twice the amount? She was already nervous about asking for such a substantial investment, and hearing it wasn't enough was like a punch to the gut. She opened her mouth to protest but stopped, realizing that now was not the time to argue.

"I will have an answer by day's end," Majid said, indicating with his hand that the meeting was over.

Once Cassidy and Yasmin were in the hallway, Cassidy said: "Wow, that was intense. How do you think I did?"

"You did as well as anyone could," Yasmin replied.

"So, what do we do now?" Cassidy asked.

"We wait."

* * *

A few hours later, Cassidy was on the jet back to California.

"Dreams aren't supposed to be easy," Yasmin said. "If they are easy, they are not dreams, they are mere tasks."

She was right, Cassidy thought as she gazed out the window as the jet took off. Dreams didn't just happen. It was up to you to *make* them happen. And the story didn't always end the way you expected.

Chapter Twenty

THE DEADLINE LOOMS

The dining room felt smaller and darker than usual. The weight of their impending deadline hanging heavy in the air. Eric, Elaine, and Reena had been working tirelessly, each of them on the phone, barely taking time to eat, with half-drunken cups of cold coffee randomly set about the room.

Less than 24 hours remained to raise the funds needed, or they would lose the 20% deposit. Forfeiting that money would be devastating.

Eric thought he could raise the money in time, but he'd exhausted every contact, and Elaine had done the same. Reena, who had no obligation to help, reached out to everyone she knew. And Cassidy, God love her, worked as hard as any salesperson Eric had ever seen, but to no avail. He'd have to break the news to her when she returned from New York.

"What do we do now?" Elaine asked. "I mean, there must be a way around it. Do we hire a lawyer?"

"We have a lawyer. She searched for a loophole, but there wasn't one. We lose the deposit and the course."

"Six-and-a-half million, just gone, with nothing to show for it?" Elaine shook her head in disbelief.

There was nothing Eric could think of to say that would make the situation better. He slammed his fist on the table. "Damn it!" he said. "We're so close. We've done everything right. Built the plan, shown the projections, poured our hearts into this, and it still isn't enough."

Reena, who had been quietly working in the corner, said, "I am starting to wonder if the course may be cursed."

Elaine shot her a look. "Not helpful, Reena."

Reena shrugged. "I mean, usually, it's the clubhouse, but I guess curses evolve."

Elaine rubbed her temples and repeated the word "cursed" under her breath. "I don't know, maybe you're right, maybe we are cursed."

"What?" Eric said. "You think we're cursed? Look at everything that's happened to us over the last 25 years. A booming business, a beautiful house, world travel, and neither of us has had a serious illness. We have each other and were blessed with the best daughter anyone could ask for. Sounds like one hell of a curse to me."

Elaine sighed. "Of course, you're right, I just..."

Elaine's cell phone buzzed.

"Who is it?" Eric asked.

"It's a text from Cassidy."

Chapter Twenty-One

CASSIDY RETURNS

Eric and Elaine sat at the dining room table in silence, the weight of failure thick in the air as the sun dipped below the horizon. In the movies, it was called the *all-is-lost scene,* and that's exactly how it felt.

All was indeed lost.

"Who died?" Cassidy asked as she walked through the door.

"God, Cassidy, we've been worried," Elaine said, jumping to her feet and hugging her. "What on Earth made you think it was okay to run off like that without telling us where you were going?"

"I told you I was going to New York," Cassidy said.

"You know what your mom means," Eric said, coming over and hugging her as well.

"Well, believe it or not, I'm an adult," Cassidy said. "But I did leave something out..."

"Go on," Eric said.

"I went to New York because I wanted to get a meeting with Yasmin Al-Hakim."

"Who's that?" Elaine asked.

"She's one of the UAE's most influential and powerful women. She was in New York, receiving an award for her work on women's rights. I thought she might be willing to be an investor in the course. Unfortunately, she didn't have the authority to invest, but she knew someone who might be interested—a billionaire businessman in Dubai named Majid Al Futtaim. And he liked the proposal."

"You sent him the proposal?" Elaine asked.

"No, I delivered it in person," Cassidy said, a smile finding its way to the corners of her mouth.

"In person?" Eric said. "How...?"

"That's where I've been for the past couple of days," Cassidy said. "I was in Riyadh."

"Riyadh?" Eric repeated in disbelief.

"You went to Dubai?" Elaine gasped. "Cassidy!"

"I was never in any danger, Mom." Cassidy rolled her eyes. "Yasmin Al-Hakim took me there on Majid's private jet. It was incredible. I am a little tired, though."

"I can't believe you did this without asking us," Eric said.

"Well, it happened very fast," Cassidy said. "And did I mention I'm an adult?"

Eric and Elaine shot each other a look, and Eric raised his hands in surrender.

"So, what happened?" Elaine asked.

"Majid said there was no way he could get involved in a project that was anything less than first class."

"Well, you tried. That's what matters," Eric said.

"Oh, I did more than try, Dad," Cassidy said, pulling an envelope from her bag and handing it to her father. "I got the money."

Eric opened the envelope and pulled out a check. Elaine took it from Eric's hand and looked at it. The check was for

$35 million.

"Majid liked the project, but he didn't like the numbers," Cassidy said. "He said they were too low, just like Reena warned us. He said we needed at least $100 million to accomplish our goals. No cutting corners. He wants Strawberry Creek to be something the whole world will notice. He wants to create a women's tournament to rival the Kia Classic."

"That is amazing, Cass, but it's too late," Eric said quietly. "The money needed to be in the bank by close of business today. The deadline has already passed."

"Oh, I know," Cassidy said. "That's why I called the partnership group yesterday and asked them to extend the deadline until noon tomorrow."

"And they said yes?" Eric said in disbelief.

"No, they were total jerks, just like you said. They wouldn't give an inch. So, I explained the situation to Majid, and he wired the money directly into their account. It got there two hours ago. We'll get the final third when we close."

Elaine's hands flew to her mouth, tears welling in her eyes, as Eric's face transformed from stunned disbelief to joy.

"I had to make three concessions though," Cassidy said. "I know you said no partners, Dad, but Majid would only sign on if you agreed to a 50-50 ownership split."

"So, we're equal partners?" Eric said, a touch of disappointment in his voice.

"No, I told him there was no deal if we didn't remain in control, so he agreed to only 40% for his end. In essence, you didn't partner with Majid, Dad—Majid partnered with *you.*"

"You said there are three concessions," Elaine said.

"Yes, Majid's organization also gets priority naming rights for ten years, with an option for another ten."

"Done," Eric said. "Hell, I'm just glad we get to keep the course. I don't care about small details."

"And Majid wants the entire sixth floor of the hotel reserved for himself and his entourage whenever they visit. But otherwise, when it's not in use, we can rent it out."

"The hotel is a go from day one?" Elaine said.

Cassidy nodded. "I told him the hotel was critical to the success of the project, and he agreed."

"This is amazing, Cass," Elaine said. "I can't believe you managed to get one of the most powerful businessmen in the world to agree to a partnership—and for 100 million dollars. How is that even possible?"

"Do you remember when I went to Dad and told him I wasn't good at selling? Dad said, 'Then don't be you.' Well, I took your advice, Dad. I decided to be someone else. *I decided to be someone who could.*"

EPILOGUE
ONE YEAR LATER

Since Cassidy's trip to the UAE, the Strawberry Creek golf course was virtually unrecognizable.

The redesign had been the priority, a task that Reena had tackled with relentless dedication. Reena also reported that her dreams had stopped. She had no idea why.

Because Eric knew his limitations, Reena became Strawberry Creek's director of operations. She was done traveling the world with her own firm but wasn't ready to retire. Eric rewarded her with a month's paid vacation to start.

As for Cassidy, she was vice president of sales, and de facto operations manager while Reena was away.

Cassidy stepped onto the hotel construction site wearing an oversized yellow hard hat, feeling the crunch of gravel beneath her boots. A group of construction engineers were waiting for her, gathered around a set of detailed plans spread across a makeshift table. She had grown familiar with these weekly walkthroughs as the project went from empty land to a bustling worksite and, now, the skeleton of a building that hinted at the luxury it would soon become.

Cassidy ran her fingers over the cool, smooth metal of the beams, remembering her father's photos from his visioning process. His dream was taking shape before her very eyes.

"Has the flooring arrived yet?" Cassidy asked.

"Yes, it arrived yesterday," the foreman said. "We'll start laying it out after the wiring is complete. We're moving faster than expected, so we're ahead of schedule."

Being ahead of schedule was music to Cassidy's ears and would make her investor in Dubai very happy. There had been so many delays in the early days, including red tape getting permits and a brutal rainy season that had turned everything into mud. Now, they were finally hitting their stride.

* * *

Cassidy's thoughts drifted to the day she boarded the plane to New York with no appointment, no real plan, and only a slim hope that Yasmin Al-Hakim would agree to talk to her. Flying across the country, uninvited, to force a meeting with someone of Yasmin's stature had been going after a *big no*.

What if she hadn't gone? What if she had played it safe, stayed home, and waited for another opportunity that might never have come? What if she had let her fear hold her back?

What if, what if, what if?

As the *"what ifs"* swirled around her, Cassidy felt a little silly. She pushed back so hard against selling. Then she remembered her dream about the older version of herself, sitting in that chair, looking out the window filled with regret and despair. She was confident that the future version of herself would never have to experience that moment.

Truthfully, Cassidy hated the sting of rejection—the tiny heartbreaks and doubts they planted. But now, she saw them for what they were: *stepping stones*. Forcing her to improve, refine her craft, and sharpen her resolve. She'd come to value them as much as the yeses, maybe even more.

No matter where life took her, Cassidy knew sales would always be a part of her, woven into how she faced the world.

And for that, she was deeply, unexpectedly grateful.

* * *

Cassidy returned to the house and found her father and mother waiting in the driveway. "Hey, we were hoping you'd get back in time," Eric said. "We're thinking of heading to Mister A's for dinner. Want to tag along?"

Cassidy's eyebrows shot up in surprise. The last time they had been at Mister A's was on the night of her graduation. Since then, things had been so hectic that there had been no time for family dinners. "Mister A's, huh?" Cassidy said. "What's the occasion?"

Elaine grinned and said: "Do we need a reason to celebrate?"

"No, we don't," Cassidy said. "I could use a good meal, but I'll come under one condition."

"Really? A condition for accepting a dinner invitation? I can't wait to hear this," Eric said.

"I get to pay," Cassidy said.

"Really?" Elaine asked. "Why?"

"Because in my twenty-two years on this planet, you've never once let me buy dinner."

Eric and Elaine glanced at each other, and they started to laugh.

"What's so funny?" Cassidy said.

"You bought us a golf course," Eric said. "Isn't that enough?"

ABOUT THE AUTHORS

Richard Fenton and **Andrea Waltz** are the bestselling authors of "Go for No!" an international phenomenon that has inspired millions to rethink their approach to rejection and success.

With over a million copies in print and translations in a dozen languages, "Go for No!" has become more than just a book—it's a movement embraced by entrepreneurs, sales professionals, and personal development enthusiasts worldwide.

As seasoned sales experts and keynote speakers, Richard and Andrea have spent decades coaching, training, and motivating sales teams across the globe.

Their work has established them as leading voices in personal and professional development, challenging people to overcome the fear of failure, embrace risk, and unlock their full potential.

Richard and Andrea have also published several other works including, When They Say No, The Go for No! Leader Workbook, The Go for No! 21-Day Challenge Workbook, The Fear Factory, Million Dollar Book Formula, and many others.

Richard and Andrea have been business and life partners for over 25 years and happily reside in the swamps of Central Florida. In their spare time, they enjoy writing fiction under the pen name, Diandra Archer. In addition to their dog, Peppers, and their cat, Storey, they have an alligator in their back pond named Gary.

Introducing the GO FOR NO!® EXPERIENCE

"The Go for No Experience" is a transformative online course that combines powerful principles, proven strategies and activities to equip you with the tools you need to succeed in business and life where receiving "no" is a daily activity! This program challenges the old models of viewing rejection, success, and achieving your goals, and shows new and counter-intuitive ways of thinking.

Designed for entrepreneurs, sales professionals, business leaders and anyone looking to break through barriers in their personal or professional life, this process is your guide to turning "no" into your greatest asset.

By the end of this course, you will:

- Learn to see "no" as a stepping stone to success, rather than a roadblock.
- Develop a mindset that welcomes rejection as an opportunity for growth and learning.
- Gain the confidence to push through setbacks, challenges and fears that have kept you from achieving your full potential.
- Master the "Go for No!" strategies to increase your sales and close more deals.
- Develop a practical, actionable plan tailored to your goals and your industry, allowing you to apply the principles of "Go for No!" immediately.

For More Information, visit GoforNo.com

www.ingramcontent.com/pod-product-compliance
Ingram Content Group UK Ltd.
Pitfield, Milton Keynes, MK11 3LW, UK
UKHW022245260325
456765UK00001B/1

9 781947 814332